ALONG THE
from
SOURCE *to* SEA

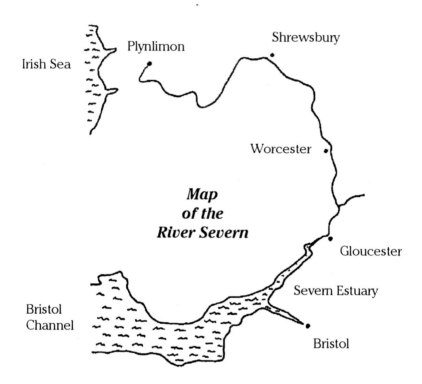

Shrewsbury

Plynlimon

Irish Sea

Worcester

*Map
of the
River Severn*

Gloucester

Severn Estuary

Bristol
Channel

Bristol

by
Chris Witts

Published
by
REARDON PUBLISHING
56, Upper Norwood Street, Leckhampton,
Cheltenham, Glos, GL53 0DU

Reardon Publishing
Copyright © 1998

Written and Researched
by
Chris Witts

ISBN 1 873877 31 5

All drawings by the author

Layout & Design
Nicholas Reardon

Cover picture Gloucester Docks
from a photograph by Nicholas Reardon

Printed by
In2Print Ltd
Cheltenham

CONTENTS

River Severn
'Britain's longest river

Introduction

In 1997 I suddenly found myself with plenty of time on my hands. What could I do that would not cost me a lot of money and not be a nuisance to others.

Walking I thought, but where? It was then that I came across an old book in my local library called The River Severn, From Source to Mouth written by M Lanchester in 1915. A fascinating little book, written in a period so different from that of today.

For sometime I had been thinking of travelling down the River Severn from the source to the sea, but lacked the inspiration. Now I had it, why not follow Lanchester's route and compare what he saw then to what is here today.

A journey such as this requires some planning, so the first thing I had to do was to purchase good maps for the whole length of the river, quite a few are required! Then a magnifying glass to study every little lane and path so that no part of the Severn is missed. I spent many a winter's evening sat by a roaring fire making notes. This was to be of great assistance later when I finally set off on my travels.

To make the trip as economical as possible I decided to camp at a couple of sites. There are good camping guides available with information on where to pitch a tent for one night or more. Time did not allow me to cover the whole trip in one journey, thus my notes were invaluable for planning how long I needed to cover certain areas. Besides retracing Lanchester's steps, I needed to be sure about changes made since his visit. This would add quite a bit of extra time on my journey.

My other interest on the Severn is the bridges that cross the river, and this would be an opportunity to photograph every one in one year, though this is another story! From the first simple wooden one that crosses the Severn, to the mighty and massive construction site of the Second Severn Crossing at Severn Beach. Some very old ones, some new ones, some barely able to take my weight, bridges of all shapes and sizes. Ugly ones, beautiful structures and some that made the mind tingle on that first sighting.

This book does not dwell on the history of the Severn as there are plenty of good books to be found on the subject. I have merely written down what I found on my journey in 1997, plus a few snippets of the past to put it all in to perspective.

Chris Witts

Chapter One
THE CONQUEST

It was a lovely summer afternoon in which to pitch a tent near the bank of the Severn at Dol-Llys Farm in Llanidloes, a good base from which to explore the source of the river.

However the fine weather was not to continue, by late afternoon it had rained continuously until the following morning. The Severn quickly rose up to bank level and then flooded over into the field, creeping perilously close to the tent, luckily it stopped a few feet from coming in. What did not stop from coming into the tent though, was the rain, eighteen hours of rain is too much for any tent to take. This obviously, is the joys of camping, especially in the Welsh hills.

Clywedog Dam

The deluge would mean that any exploration of the source of the Severn in the Plynlimon hills would be out of the question for a few days. Never mind, there is the Clywedog Dam to visit. Lanchester would have been amazed to see what a transformation this area has gone through. At a height of 237 feet it is Britain's highest dam, completed in 1967, it extends for 6 miles through the Bryn Tail Gorge. Built to control flood water in winter and to regulate the flow of water in the lower reaches of the Severn during the summer period. A magnificent feat of engineering, Lanchester would have been impressed, but what would he have seen now lying under 11,000,000,000 gallons of water? In this area during the 19th century were sixteen lead mines, one has been preserved as a monument at the foot of the Clywedog Dam, the Bryn Tail mine.

Following two days of sunshine it was decided to make an early attempt to climb Plynlimon in an attempt to find the source. Life has been made easier for the walker today than when Lanchester did it in 1915. Now the car can be left at the picnic site of the Hafren Forest tourist trail. There are even signs pointing the walker in the right direction! A stranger to the area may be misled by how inviting it is to walk along the trail, through the forest and on up to the source. To go to the source requires good weather and a lot of stamina, it could be quite frightening to get caught on the top of Plynlimon in bad weather.

It was a sultry morning, wet under foot, yet warm in the air. The plan was to follow the Severn as much as possible, not easy as the river is only a couple of feet wide and there are other streams flowing down the hill. To make it more difficult the Severn in this area is known as Afon Hafren, so considerable concentration is required to keep on the right track. In Lanchester's day he would have been walking through bare grassland, now it is a vast forest of Norwegian trees, grown here since 1937.

The climb up amongst the trees was becoming very steep, shoes sinking down into the mud. Was this the peat bog that is wet and swamp like, even in the driest weather, that gave Lanchester problems on his climb to the summit? The only way to climb up now was to pull oneself from tree to tree, one false move and it would have been a dangerous quick descent to the bottom. The flies are a problem too, thousands of them sticking to all exposed parts of the body. Patience wears thin as they have to be continually swiped with a hanky. Suddenly, coming out into a clearing could be seen the famous Blaen Hafren Falls.

Pictures of the falls make them look more spectacular than they actually are, but it does provide a good spot to have some lunch, even if the flies try to share the sandwiches as well. From the falls there is a path leading on up the hill, but it became too difficult to penetrate the thick foliage. This left no option but to look for another way up the steep slope through the forest. The forest ends at the edge of a large, clear expanse of moorland, a peat bog that can be negotiated with care. The single path leads forever up, a long climb to one summit, only to be confronted by another long climb to the next! Although the air was becoming fresher, the flies were still following and causing considerable irritation. Another hour would pass before the final summit would be reached.

The ground takes on more of a dry feel as the summit becomes closer. When at last the summit is reached it has numerous piles of slate rock and pools of dark, black water. Dark because of the peat. There are no signs to inform the walker that they at the source of the River Severn, just as there are no streams of water to indicate where the river begins, in fact it all happens beneath the peat and rock. It is difficult to imagine that this is the start of Britain's longest river, two hundred and twenty miles from here, to the estuary as it becomes the Bristol Channel.

The view is superb, surrounded by other high peaks; could that be the mountain range of Snowdonia in the distance? Great Britain is thought of as a small island, yet here one can be alone in a totally lonely and hostile environment, not a car, house or anything of the twentieth century to be seen! It does not pay to stop and ponder too long whilst on the summit, for storm clouds can quickly close in and cover the area in a thick mist. Plynlimon in a storm is not recommended, as this is dangerous country, with no shelter.

Walking back down the hill is obviously a lot easier than the climb had been up to the summit. When the forest is reached the walker can take the road back towards the picnic site, this route is harder on the feet and quite uninteresting, but better than facing what could be a dangerous steep path through the trees. About a mile from the car park is located the first official bridge to cross the River Severn. A new bridge built in 1992, it is constructed of good quality timber and no doubt will last for a long time. At this point the Severn has already fallen 1,000 feet from the source, cascading down, tumbling over boulders with the spirit of a new born animal. The water is so crystal clear, yet the banks amongst the plant life display a colour of yellow ochre, this from the ore in the ground.

Hafren Forest

The First official bridge over the River Severn

Chapter Two
DOWN TO NEWTOWN

From the first bridge the Severn is running very fast, falling all the time, twisting and turning on its way down through the Hafren Forest. The Forestry Commission maintain the forest trail to a high standard, even laying a considerable length of duckboarding across a wet area. Although the river has only the width of a narrow stream, it is difficult to cross because of the soft mud either side of the banks. There are a couple of footbridges provided, one just being a plank supported by scaffold poles, another one built recently of stone and timber. Due to the dangerous condition of path and bridge, the Forestry Commission have closed off part of one walk, but this shouldn't deter the walker from enjoying a splendid day exploring the large Hafren Forest.

It is a small road that leads the traveller back to Llanidloes, first passing a small cottage at Rhyd-yr-Onnen. This delightful old cottage is the first sign of life to be seen, albeit in a lonely, quite spooky spot, now habitated by an elderly couple from the Midlands who have only recently moved here. From the hustle and bustle of commerce to the complete solitude of the country, their only contact with human life is the daily visit by the postman.

Nothing has changed here since Lanchester came in 1915, apart from the view back towards the source. In his day it was barren countryside, now full of trees of the Hafren Forest. The road continues on down, passing several old farms, the farmer suspicious of anyone who stops and tries to engage him in a conversation. There are some forestry houses at Tan Hinon, but again conversation was difficult with the occupiers. It would appear that the Severn plays no part in their lives, just a stream taken for granted that it will be there tomorrow and every day after that.

The road moves away from the river and passes through countryside as peaceful now as it always has been down through the centuries. An old chapel nestles in the hill side, looking derelict, not though, like the one at the hamlet of Old Hall, which stands proudly on the side of the Severn. New and old cottages here blend well together, having been built close to the plain concrete bridge which crosses the river, the only disappointing structure in the hamlet. Not like the next village of Glan-y-Nant, with its numerous houses sprawling through the area. Located down a track is a steel footbridge, not very old, but it would seem to be going nowhere. From the track it crossed the river and vanished into a thick coppice. Shortly before arriving at Llanidloes is the village of Mount Severn with its traditional stone bridge, a pity that it is so well hidden amongst foliage and bracken.

Ten miles from the source is the town of Llanidloes. The first appearance of the town as it is approached from Mount Severn is not very pleasing to the eye, an old mill and a row of houses, all backing onto the river. The houses and mill are separated by one of the two stone bridges that cross the river in the town. Located about a quarter of a mile apart, this first one is Short Bridge, designed by Thomas Penson and built in 1849. Penson is well known for designing the iron bridges of Montgomeryshire in the nineteenth century.

Proceeding over Short Bridge the view of Llanidloes changes dramatically, there in the distance is the old Market Hall, dating from about 1600, it is the only one of its kind remaining in Wales. This is a good place to begin to explore the town, for this is now the museum, giving the visitor the full history since the granting of a charter to the town in 1280. Llanidloes is now bypassed by a new road which thankfully is taking away large volumes of traffic. It must have been an unpleasant place to live in before the bypass was opened, for a town of this age was never designed to cope with our modern traffic.

The town boasts a mixture of red brick and grey stone properties. Once there was a flourishing wool trade here, now that has been lost to Bradford in Yorkshire. The old mills have now been converted for use by the modern entrepreneur. A short riverside path leads to the Church of St. Idloes, noted for its magnificent roof with each hammerbeam adorned with a winged angel. On the opposite side of the river from the church enters the River Clywedog into the Severn. Here the Clywedog looks unimportant, but only two miles up its course is the massive dam.

The second bridge in Llanidloes is the Long Bridge, built in the first half of the nineteenth century to replace an ancient and dangerous wooden structure. Back in 1798 a chap called Henry Skrine saw this old wooden bridge and stated that it should be replaced. It was so bad that it was safer to ford the river than cross the bridge

Long Bridge
Llanidloes

and that is just what the locals used to do, except when the river was in flood. The Severn does not play a big part in life at Llanidloes today, except that the town has provided the lovely walk along the river, close to the church.

One of the delights of camping at Dol-Lys Farm is the marvellous walks along the river bank on wonderful summer evenings with the sun low in the sky, reflecting in the clear water of the Severn. As the river leaves Llanidloes it passes through some lovely meadows, with sheep and cattle gently grazing on rich green pastures. Looking skyward to the east there is a view which would have shocked Lanchester. Acres and acres of windmills on top of the distant hills, not the traditional type, but those new tall metal ones, designed for generating electricity. There are twenty four 300 kw wind turbines on top of Myndd-y-Cemais, capable of producing enough electricity to supply more than 6,500 homes.

An hour soon passes when walking in such beautiful surroundings, time to reflect on the past. How did Lanchester travel through this area, did he walk along this path or did he keep to the road which runs parallel with the river? He did question as to why did the Severn give its name to the whole river and not the Clywedog? After all, before the dam was built the River Clywedog drained a large area and brought more water down to Llanidloes than did the Severn. His conclusion was, that it was due to the Severn rising some four hundred feet above the Clywedog.

Lanchester has a drawing in his book of a wooden bridge located somewhere between Llanidloes and Llandinam, could this be the old railway bridge that now lay derelict in a thick coppice? Even the local farmer's wife was sure that this bridge had long disappeared, but there it was, unsafe and close to falling down. For the whole length of the River Severn are natural floodplains where nature allows the water in the river to overspill and lay in the fields until the river level drops. This area is no exception, for after a spell of heavy rain more water would come down from the hills than the river could carry, causing flooding in places. Although Lanchester explored the Severn in the summer when there was not much water running over the pebbles, local schoolchildren described to him what the floods were really like in winter. The river would resemble a large lake, some years worse than others. Perhaps then, this bridge will not last many more winters before it to becomes a casualty of a flood.

The busy A470 trunk road from Llanidloes to Llandinam follows the Severn for much of the way, twisting and turning, with drivers impatient should they find themselves stuck behind slow moving traffic. A large layby is provided near Upper Penrhuddlan complete with mobile cafe, a welcome for the weary traveller. From the layby a small road crosses the Severn over Dolwen Bridge, built of concrete in 1926, it does have iron railings, so was there an iron bridge on this site at one time?

A strange phenomenon of the Severn is that from the source its course is north up to Shrewsbury and then twists and turns until it begins to run its course south. Look at any atlas and you will see that the source lies slightly above Worcester! This explains why it takes approximately 36 hours for water to reach the estuary, yet water from the source of the Wye, which is also at Plynlimon, will take only a day to travel its course down to the Severn Estuary.

Farther down the A470 is Llandinam, a pretty village spoilt by the busy road which separates it from the river. Although not much has changed since Lanchester passed through, in 1988 Llandinam was

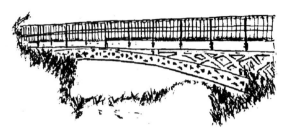

Llandinam Bridge, Llandinam

the winner of the Wales in Bloom competition. The Severn is crossed by Llandinam Bridge, which, when built in 1843 was the first iron bridge to be erected in Montgomeryshire. It was designed by the county surveyor, Thomas Penson, who was also responsible for three other iron bridges that cross the river in the county. At the A470 trunk road end of the bridge stands a large statue of David Davies, [1818 - 1890]. As a nineteenth century industrialist, who first taught at the local school, he was to prosper and become one of the leading figures in the development of mines and railways in South Wales. One of his first commercial undertakings was to build the approach roads and abutments for Penson's bridge.

Due to the Severn being subjected to flooding in this area, a high stone embankment was built to protect the ancient village of Llandinam from being swept away. Much of the land that the Severn flows through here is only just above river level, so the bank has been artificially raised to protect much of it, but the meadows still became flooded last century as they still do today. Being a natural floodplain there has never been many cottages built on the low ground, those inhabitants that do live on it take it for granted that their property will be subjected to flooding.

A mile down the river is the old Roman settlement of Caersws, important in its day, but now just an average village. It does boast a railway junction though, with the track crossing the river on a bridge built of timber. In 1868 during a severe flood, the railway embankment was carried away, taking a train from Newtown with it, killing the driver and fireman. Passengers in those days complained that they had to trundle their luggage along a muddy path for half a mile from the station to the road into Caersws. Today the muddy path is still there, but now passengers drive in their cars from the station into Caersws.

Caersws Bridge, which was built of stone in 1821, carries the A470 road across the Severn into the village. Lanchester had little to say about the village, perhaps he was keeping clear of controversy, not like Leland and Edward Lhwyd. They did not have a good word to say about Caersws, except to say the ale is good and the landladies handsome.

The river continues to wander down through water meadows before being restricted at the town of Newtown. It is now the busy A489 that travels from Caersws to Newtown, in most parts moving away from the river. As the road passes through the hamlet of Red House an attractive footbridge can be seen across a field. This is Festival Footbridge, a suspension type bridge built in 1951 by Montgomeryshire County Council, to a design by David Rowell & Company of Westminster. It was allowed to fall into a derelict state, but has recently been restored to its original glory, standing in isolation, not a soul to be seen.

Newtown is approached through new housing estates and small industrial units. The river is difficult to locate and even harder to find someone who can explain how it can be found. One local pointed to a field and claimed, in a not too positive tone, that the Severn could be found at the far end. Wrong, after spending a wasted twenty minutes negotiating the car in a none too level field. The best way to see the river is to drive to the car park near the bus station and council offices, then walk along the good footpath which follows the Severn all the way through the town.

Lanchester didn't stay long at Newtown, only long enough to see a couple of small punts moored amongst the bushes. Nothing like that was to be seen today, not even a coracle. For this is coracle country, a type of round boat made with a frame of basket-work covered inside and out with stout canvas well tarred. They looked like large walnut shells and were difficult to manage, as they were easily upset. These strange craft date back to the Ancient Britons, but even in 1915 there were very few to be seen. Today not one is to be seen in regular use on the river, only the enthusiast, who also arranges special events where they may give demonstrations to the public.

During the reign of Edward I Newtown became an established market town. A flourishing street market fills the main street every Tuesday, a tradition that began 700 years ago. This town has a magical feel about it, it may be small in size, but turn a corner and there is some little gem to be explored. A replica of a W. H. Smith shop from the 1920's with a museum above, delightful tea shops with delicious cream teas and the Church of St David's, built by Thomas Penson in 1847. Lanchester missed so much by not allowing himself more time to explore this small market town.

It is not only the lowly mortal who found Newtown such a delight to visit. Royalty has spent time here to, King Charles stayed here in 1645 and our present Prince of Wales made an official visit to the town in 1969. Newtown does not live in the past though, for it boasts an impressive new bridge crossing the Severn and linking the town to the satellite district of Llanllwchaiarn.

Llanllwchaiarn is a town in its own right, quite different in appearance to Newtown, with a tight huddle of three and four storey blocks built on streets which run at right angles to each other. Dark, mysterious archways lead into courts and alleys hidden amongst the blocks. Only 150 years ago this area was a thriving industrial centre, full of wool factories operating from the top floors of many of the blocks. Perhaps this is why Lanchester hurried through the town? Long Bridge, another of Thomas Penson's bridges, which was built in 1826, was until recently the only communicating link between the two towns. The footpath was added 30 years later in 1857, it was very cleverly suspended on iron brackets, and to the casual observer would appear to have been the original part of the bridge. To a great relief of those who had to suffer the horrors of modern traffic, Powys County Council had the Newtown Bypass Bridge built in 1993.

It is not only the relief of traffic that Newtown now enjoys, it has, hopefully, seen the last of the floods that the town used to suffer. There were bad floods in 1936, 1947, 1960 and 1964. For this reason a successful flood defence scheme was constructed in 1967 by raising the height of the river banks. Unfortunately water has to go somewhere and it would appear that areas farther down the Severn now suffer floods more regularly.

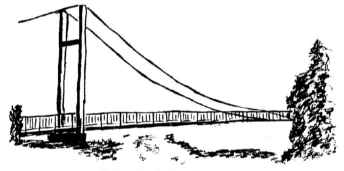

Dolerw Footbridge, Newtown

A pleasant walk along the Severn is through Dolerw Park, this also boasts a new bridge. The Dolerw Park Footbridge was built in 1973 and is almost a replica of the M4 Severn Suspension Bridge. To see more of the river at Newtown requires a slight spirit of adventure! It took an hour to locate the now disused Glanhafren Halt Railway Station on the Llanllwchaiarn side of the river, down an old track towards the railway line built in a cutting. The old halt station house is now occupied by an elderly couple who are not used to seeing strangers, least of all visitors who only want to see the Severn. It now requires a quick, but difficult struggle through brambles to find the railway bridge that crosses the river, disappointment because there is not much to see of the river, but at least it was found.

Time now to leave Newtown and explore more of the river towards Shrewsbury.

Chapter Three
TO THE WELSH BORDER

The A483 trunk road continues out of Newtown, following the railway line for a few miles towards Welshpool. Quickly passing a mixture of small industrial units and housing the road is soon out into the open countryside. The traffic though is still heavy and fast, but look out for the turning to Aberbechan, for it is worth making the left turn at the junction to view an idyllic scene of the Severn. An old stone bridge crosses the river at this point, where, with care, the car can be parked whilst a walk onto the bridge offers a view of the river peacefully running its course towards England. A few minutes spent here can recharge the mind before facing that hustle and bustle of traffic again. It would appear that Lanchester did not spend too much time in this area, as he only makes a brief mention of the canal. It is from here that the Shropshire Union Canal follows the Severn downstream for a considerable distance. The upper limit for navigation in the 18th century was to Pool Quay, just below Welshpool, so a canal was built for trade to reach Newtown. The canal has been allowed to become derelict and overgrown for a great many years, but now with the enthusiasm of willing volunteers is slowly being brought back to life.

As the trunk road approaches Abermule the driver has the choice of either continuing on the bypass, built in 1975, or to take the original road through the village. A good excuse to take the old road is the opportunity of visiting the county town of Montgomery. The road sign points away from the Severn, giving a distance of two miles to the town and a long two miles it is! The drive is worth it though, for as the car turns into Broad Street a wonderful view of the old town hall set in the original mediaeval street plan greets the tired driver. For the less able bodied a drive up the hill to the ruins of Montgomery Castle is a must. Choose a summer lunch-time when the happy noise of children floats up in the air from the school below. Admire the magnificent panoramic scenery, at the same time reflecting of what great men have stood at this same spot down through the centuries. Whilst in this very small town it would be a pity to leave it without first taking refreshments at either the tea shoppe or hostelry before facing the busy A483 trunk road again.

Between Abermule and Welshpool there are several interesting bridges that cross the Severn. At Abermule is Brynderwen Bridge, designed by Thomas Penson in 1852 and built by the Brymbo Company of Wrexham. It has written on it, "THIS SECOND IRON BRIDGE CONSTRUCTED IN THE COUNTY OF MONTGOMERY WAS ERECTED IN THE YEAR 1852". Another of Penson's iron bridges is the Caer Howel Bridge, built a little later in 1858. Unfortunately it now is suffering from the ravages of time, for a temporary Bailey Bridge has had to have been constructed on top of the original.

Between Abermule and Caer Howel with a little exploration can be found the old Fron Footbridge. Another of David Rowell's suspension footbridges built in 1926, one end lay hidden in overgrown bushes, the other on the edge of a corn field. Now looking non too safe and covered in rust, how long before it also falls foul of time? Again this was another footbridge that seems to go nowhere. No doubt, back in 1926, the scene was a lot different with communities on both sides of the river requiring to cross the river here.

The river continues to travel north, passing the market town of Welshpool before turning in an easterly direction towards Shrewsbury. Welshpool lies a couple of miles from the Severn and is an old town steeped in history. Monday is market day and the town is alive with farmers with their cattle at the local cattle market. Watch these men during the afternoon, standing on street corners discussing the morning sale. Their faces telling all whether they had a good sale or not.

For the modern tourist Welshpool makes an ideal base with which to explore the surrounding countryside. There is much to see, including the Welshpool & Llanfair Light Railway and the Shropshire Union Canal. Both are located in the town, each attractive to the tourist.

At Buttington the canal follows the Severn for a number of miles towards Pool Quay. During the summer months small boats can be seen travelling along the canal, although, at parts having to struggle through large amounts of weeds. Over the centuries numerous battles have taken place on the land around Welshpool, including in 894 A.D. one between the Danes and the Welsh at Buttington.

Pool Quay conjures up a vision of the river with landing stage complete with crane for the loading of vessels. Nothing could be farther from the truth! It is true to say that this was the upper limit on the Severn that trading vessels could navigate to, but that was a long time ago. Even Lanchester in his book states that when standing on the weedgrown bank it is difficult to realize that this was a busy place to see barges unloading their cargoes. He thinks that there was more water in the river than there is today, but still the thirty ton barges would have had a long and tedious journey to get to Pool Quay. They would then have a long wait for the right conditions before making the return trip back down the river.

All roads now leave the river in peace until the B4393 crosses the Severn at Llandrinio. From here can be seen Breidden Hill rising dramatically out of the landscape. Lanchester made the effort to climb to the top for he mentions the Severn winding like a silver ribbon through the countryside. Could he see Breidden Hill today he would be amazed to see the array of large radio aerials perched precariously on the top. It would appear that man through the ages has left one mark or another on this great hill, from Bronze Age implements to Admiral Rodney's pillar of the 18th century.

Llandrinio Bridge, Llandrinio

Llandrinio Bridge is a narrow, steeply arched structure built in 1775 of ruddy coloured stone. One of the handsomest bridges to cross the Severn, at a point where the river turns eastward for the last two miles before crossing the border into England.

The river now forms part of the boundary line between Wales and England, a boundary which twists and turns, confusing the tourist as to what country they are in! Lanchester mentions that this part of the river used to be subjected to particular bad floods, especially the village of Melverley which lies on the River Vyrnwy just above the junction with the Severn. There is a large dam at Lake Vyrnwy which regulates the amount of water in the river below thus eliminating some of the flooding problems.

Just below the junction of the two rivers is Crewgreen bridge. Built in 1947 as a railway bridge for the Criggion branch of the Shropshire and Montgomery Railway for carrying War Emergency materials. British Rail had planned to demolish it in 1962, but the bridge was purchased in-situ by Shropshire County Council and converted to a road bridge.

For a final view of Wales stand at this border on a cold, sunny winters day and look back at the Welsh mountains capped with snow. This will be a reminder of the birth of the mighty Severn, rising from peat bogs of Plynlimon and now already taking command of the countryside by dictating its course.

Chapter Four
SHREWSBURY AND BEYOND

Even with the modern motor car and still ten miles to go before arriving at Shrewsbury, the journey is becoming weary. So far in his book, Lanchester makes no mention of how he travelled or where he stayed at night. Back in 1915 travel was a lot slower and the choice of accommodation must have been limited. No B&Bs, camp sites or Tourist Offices where a bed for the night can be found and booked. For the weary traveller, Shrewsbury makes the ideal place to stop for the night, the local Tourist Office will find and book a room for you, but make sure you arrive before they close!

Before arriving at Shrewsbury though, time must be spent at Montford Bridge, admiring the old and the new. The village now boasts a new bypass, built in 1992 it carries a modern bridge over the Severn. Prior to the opening of this bypass all traffic had to negotiate the 18th century red sandstone bridge across the river.

Montford Bridge

Designed by Thomas Telford, it was built by John Carline and John Tilley and opened in 1792. The bridge was damaged in 1963, not by heavy traffic, but by frost. The decking was widened with reinforced concrete and parapets replaced with wrought iron railings.

Montford Bypass Bridge

The medieval town of Shrewsbury deserves some time in exploring it, with many of the old properties preserved and over a thousand listed buildings to see. The town boasts a castle, a prison designed by Telford and a fine looking railway station built over the Severn. The river almost surrounds the town, failing by only a couple of hundred yards, this makes it confusing for the first time visitor to get their bearings. Only one thing spoils this fine old town, the huge amount of modern traffic. Nose to tail through the streets all day and every day, so bad that the smell of exhaust fumes on a hot day makes it quite unbearable. One way to escape this noise and smell is to walk along the river bank, starting at Frankwell Footbridge, a cable stayed suspension bridge built in 1979 to link the large car-park with the bus station and shopping centre. The pleasant walk along the river footpath will take you past some interesting bridges, old and new, including Welsh Bridge of 1795, Kingsland Toll Bridge of 1881 and the English Bridge of 1768. Numerous signs point to an area known as the Quarry, don't be put off, this is a lovely park with splendid views of some grand buildings. A large statue of Sabrina, Goddess of the Severn, is located in the park, set in a delightful small garden of flowers, trees and waterfalls.

As you reach Castle Bridge, the last of the town bridges, climb up the steep steps which will bring you to Shrewsbury Prison. Admire the architecture and then walk across the road to the covered walkway which leads to the railway station. Another wonderful piece of architecture, again worth a few moments to stand and admire before attempting the short, hard walk up to the castle which was founded in the 1080s by Roger de Montgomery. The castle gardens with their floral beauty are well worth a walk around and are open to the public.

Shrewsbury is a fascinating place to visit, certainly with the tourist visitor in mind. Perhaps the buildings are artificially preserved with modern shopping companies now occupying them, but let your mind wander and the past can come to life. We have the benefits of the twentieth century without the smells of sewage in the streets, the people dying young from incurable diseases, only a few fortunate to gain any kind of education. Yet at the end of the walk around the town the traffic takes priority over everything, with impatient motorists revving their engines and blowing of horns.

Traffic chaos, even though a new large bypass was opened around Shrewsbury in 1992, with three large flyovers crossing the Severn.

The one thing that Lanchester mentions was the boating on the river, small motor launches and rowing boats. Today the same boats can still be seen on the river, which must be the highest point on the Severn that this type of boat can be seen. It is a pity though that Lanchester didn't mention other forms of transport, as the motor car or pony and trap. It would appear from reading history books that this country has never been free of traffic chaos and perhaps never will be!

Four miles south east of Shrewsbury is the village of Atcham. Here is the site of the first of the preserved Severn bridges, John Gwynn's bridge of 1776, now standing as a national monument. A new bridge was built in 1927 with a span of 450 feet with open spandrel reinforced concrete arches. It was officially opened on the 24th October 1929 by The Minister of Transport, Herbert Morrison, M.P.

Lanchester mentions the Roman occupation of Wroxeter and the subsequent destruction done by the Saxons. Today the motorist will see little to remind him of that time long ago in the books of history, in fact there is not a lot to see until Cressage is reached. Cressage Bridge was being rebuilt when Lanchester passed through in 1913. The new reinforced structure replaced an old wooden bridge and he went into great detail of how this most up-to-date bridge was being built. From here he had a good view of the Wrekin as is the same today. The Wrekin looks dramatic with a backdrop of black snow clouds with shafts of sunlight lighting up the top of the hill.

The ruins of Buildwas Abbey is the next significant site to be reached on the journey down the Severn. It lay in ruins in Lanchester's day as they do today, now a tourist attraction with the area constantly being landscaped to please the visitor. He mentioned the iron bridge built in 1905 to replace the one built by Telford in 1796. This site has seen quite a few bridges and for various reasons they don't seem to last very long. Telford's bridge was built to replace one that had been swept away in the great floods of 1795 and the one of 1905 has already been replaced by a new bridge built by Shropshire County Council in 1992. In 1773 there occurred at this spot a violent earthquake that caused part of the wooded hillside to fall into the river. This would have surely weakened the foundation of any bridge built here.

From Buildwas Lanchester travels through Coalbrookdale, Ironbridge and Coalport. This is an area that he would not recognise today, only three miles long, but what a change. The huge red cooling towers of Ironbridge Power Station on the opposite side of the river, first built in 1932, with a second Power Station built in 1963, belching out

*Ironbridge
Power Station*

Iron Bridge

large white clouds into the atmosphere. A coal fired station, it now receives tonnes of coal by rail across the beautiful Albert Edward Railway Bridge.

This is tourist country with the now preserved Iron Bridge the centre attraction. Built in 1779 by Darby III at his works in nearby Coalbrookdale it is the first cast iron bridge ever to have been built. During the 1970s major work was undertaken to restore the bridge. This involved constructing an inverted concrete arch in the river bed to keep the abutments apart. This is an area that does justify more than a fleeting visit, at least a few days to explore the surrounding district. In fact the whole area has been turned into one large museum from, according to legend, very dirty, run down villages.

These villages now come under the one name of Telford. A new, very modern town has been built a few miles from Ironbridge and named after the great man himself, Thomas Telford. Because there is so much to see here it was decided to make this a base for a few days and camp in the tent. It was not difficult to find a suitable site, halfway between the river and

Telford Shopping Centre with statue of Thomas Telford

Telford centre, surrounded by a fast new road system which is rather daunting to the first time visitor, but marvellous to use having got one's bearings. Telford could be described as a red brick and concrete jungle, but it does seem to work, with large free car parks and under cover shopping malls.

Entering the town of Bridgnorth

The next town of any size on the Severn is Bridgnorth. A town with history dating back long before the Norman Conquest, much would have changed since then, but not necessarily much since Lanchester was here. There is still the Leaning Tower of the old castle standing in the park at the top of the hill and Stoneway Steps still link the Low Town with the High Town. Close to the Stoneway Steps is the famous Cliff Railway, the country's steepest and shortest inland railway. This had only been open a short while when Lanchester paid a visit to the town, he noticed that the local population didn't like using it, they would still prefer the long climb up the steps.

This is another town with numerous listed buildings, the Northgate, the Town Hall and more recently preserved is the Severn Valley Railway, for steam railway buffs, a great attraction. The market town sits high on a red sandstone ridge overlooking the River Severn and until the last century was a thriving river port. The main street is lined with Victorian shop fronts with half timbered buildings, whilst the sandstone cliffs below are honeycombed with caves once inhabited by dwellers. Castle Walk commands fine views of the Severn which one prominent visitor, King Charles I proclaimed was the finest in his

Bridgnorth

Kingdom. Not only was Thomas Telford a great bridge designer, but he also designed the Church of St. Mary Magdalene with its graceful domed tower in 1792. Bridgnorth is definitely the Jewel of the Severn.

Lanchester visited Hampton Lode to view the old ferry which still operates today. He said it was a horse ferry, but now two elderly ladies work it and apparently have done so for quite a few years. He also visited Arley which had a ferry too, but that was replaced by a footbridge in 1971.

Something that Lanchester and today's visitor would not have seen was the colliery at Alveley. Opened in 1939 the colliery supplied coal to Stourport Power Station, which was transported there in wagons on trains on the Severn Valley Railway. The colliery closed in 1969.

At last Lanchester makes mention of places to stay for the night. Below Arley the Wyre Forest lies on the right bank of the river with tents to be seen in the fields and later, cottages and farms providing tea and lodgings. This area was fairly accessible to people from the Midlands, which they treated as a weekend resort for boating and fishing parties. He also makes mention of the Severn Pipe Bridge at Trimpley, some two miles above Bewdley. This magnificent bridge was built for the sole purpose of carrying water across the Severn from the Elan Valley at Rhayader to Birmingham.

The market town of Bewdley is situated on the right bank of the Severn and iike Bridgnorth, steeped in history. Barges of seventy tonnes could be seen trading here until the last century, now only rowing boats and dinghies can be seen. It was a tough time trying to navigate the barges up the river, they would have to be pulled either by horse or by men and then only if the river level was deep enough. Some would spend weeks waiting for the river to rise before being able to move the barges.

Today whilst visiting this Worcestershire Georgian town the sound of a steam whistle may be heard in the distance. This will be one of the steam engines on the preserved Severn Valley Railway leaving Bewdley Station on it's climb up the bank towards Bridgnorth. Another venue that Lanchester would have found fascinating is the West Midland Safari Park, located a short distance from the town. What would he have made of driving around in a motor car with wild animals such as monkeys, giraffes and lions roaming around you? In his day it was very much the municipal zoo with all animals firmly locked in cages!

If river trade was to continue on the Severn something would have to be done to make it easier for vessels to get up the river. It was decided therefore, in the middle of the nineteenth century to canalize the river up as far as Stourport.

Chapter Five
MIDDLE SEVERN NAVIGATION

Stourport on Severn is not a pretty town, but it does have an interesting past, well worth spending a few hours exploring it. The river takes on a dramatic change as it flows beneath Stourport Bridge. Above the bridge the Severn still retains that look of grandeur, gracefully flowing through unspoilt countryside, far from any main highway. Not only is the change visually noticeable downstream of the bridge, but there is a sense of change in the air. The river now becomes a commercial waterway, for the navigation system of the Severn begins at Stourport, the highest point on the river that craft officially trade to.

In his book, Lanchester also comments on the commercial river traffic that traded to the town, barges being towed by modern steam tugs. Had he visited Stourport during the thirty years between 1930 and 1960 he would have seen the river full of craft carrying various types of cargoes, from timber to canned food, with large fleets of oil tanker barges bringing petroleum from Avonmouth. Now all this has ceased, the oil comes by pipeline and other goods are carried on huge juggernauts which clog up our road system.

Still remaining to remind us of this commercial waterway are the quay walls where the vessels would unload their cargoes. On the right bank below the bridge is a repair yard still with its slipway where small craft, like a river tug, can be hauled out of the water for repair. On the opposite bank is a hideous fun fair, quite a shock when first observed, but remember, people come from the Midlands for a day out in Stourport, to let their hair down and enjoy themselves. Below the fun fair is where the canal system enters the Severn, this the reason why Stourport was developed into a bustling town.

James Brindley, the great canal builder, in 1771 completed the Staffordshire and Worcestershire Canal. John Wesley the preacher visited the town six years after the opening of the canal and noticed it was still only a small village, twenty years later he commented that it had grown into a large town.

Below the canal complex can still be seen the oil terminal where the tanker barges would discharge their volatile cargo of oil. Now with that trade gone, along with the closure of the coal fired power station, all that remains are the classic small industrial units of our time. There is however a large boat yard operating here, together with a small marina. Look carefully and converted commercial barges can be seen in use as private craft, as homes or for other work. One enterprising company operates two old tanker barges as pleasure craft, giving trips down to Worcester on the CARBOLATE and RIVER KING.

As mentioned previously the River Severn was canalized in the middle of the nineteenth century to allow commercial vessels to trade up as far as Stourport. The Severn is naturally a shallow river apart from when a period of rain causes the river level to rise as the extra water flows down from the Welsh hills. This extra rise in the river level is known as "Fresh Water". To make the river stay at a permanent level, seven weirs were built at locations between Stourport and Gloucester, but as vessels cannot sail over these weirs locks had to be built as well. The first one below Stourport is Lincomb Lock, located at the foot of a red sandstone cliff, the last of these to be seen on our journey down the river.

The river regains some of its splendour as it flows down towards Holt Fleet Lock and below one of Telford's classic bridges. Away from the river the roads are still busy with the never-ending great volumes of traffic. Unfortunately the river is beginning to suffer the same as boat ownership and hiring becomes easier. The impatient car driver becomes the impatient boatman in his boat on the river, racing to be first at the locks. Bevere Lock is next, just a few miles above Worcester. This is an award winning lock, not a stone out of place, flowers in full bloom, hedges clipped to perfection. The British Waterways Board control the navigation on the Severn between Stourport and Sharpness as well as many canal and river systems in the United Kingdom. Each year they hold the customary "Best Kept Lock" competition, if not winning the title, Bevere Lock usually comes a close second.

Worcester, the first city on the Severn and as to be expected full of people either enjoying a day at the shops or going about their business life. The river first passes Worcester Racecourse and the enterpris-

Worcester during the floods

ing council allows it to be used as a car park on non race days. It then flows beneath three different types of bridges, a very modern footbridge, the railway bridge and the very old Worcester Bridge. Opened in 1781, it has had a few alterations made to it since then, the last was in 1930, when a complete reconstruction took place.

Lanchester commented on it as does everyone who visits the town, the Cathedral. Built alongside the left bank of the river, it makes a superb backdrop to the Severn, together with the other ancient buildings that surround it. From the railway bridge it is possible to walk along the river bank which must be classed as one of the best town walks on the Severn. The walk follows the river until Diglis Lock, passing the Cathedral, the Royal Worcester Porcelain Works and the entrance to the Worcester and Birmingham Canal. It also passes Diglis Basin, something that Lanchester would not have seen, the very large seagoing tanker barges unloading oil products such as petrol, diesel and heavy black oil for industry.

During the 1950s and 60s these tankers would bring petroleum products from as far as Swansea carrying up to 400 tonnes of cargo. Struggling up the Severn in the summer, scraping the bottom of the river, taking seven hours from Gloucester, which only takes thirty minutes in a car. Crewed by four men, these tankers formed a floating pipeline on the river, operating from five in the morning until ten at night. During the hours of darkness headlights would be fitted on the bow of each vessel to enable them to see where the bank was. Yet the people of Worcester took little notice of these tankers, that is until they couldn't buy petrol for the car because the oil depot was running short. Now the only commercial vessel to be seen is a small tug of the British Waterways fleet, large pleasure boats of the Worcester Steamboat Company or the OLIVER CROMWELL.

Recently an enterprising businessman could see a market to run a hotel vessel taking passengers on a weekly holiday from Sharpness to Worcester. He built his own craft in the style of a Mississippi steamboat and planned to name it THE DUKE OF GLOUCESTER, but protocol forbade him to do that. So he decided on the name of OLIVER CROMWELL, historically an enemy of the Royalists. This large stern wheeler is a tight fit in the locks at Gloucester and Worcester, as well as having little room left when going under the bridges.

Before leaving Worcester a reminder of what Lanchester would have seen then and the difference today. Apart from more modern river craft, the oil jetties and tanks, he would not see a lot of change, certainly the Cathedral will always be there and hopefully the buildings around it. A modern town, but has still been able to retain a lot of the old to remind us of the past, the planners have coped well with taking it into the twenty-first century.

Between Worcester and Upton upon Severn the scenery has changed little, the river still passes through rich fertile meadows and orchard land. To the right of the river can be seen good views of the dramatic range of the Malvern Hills with the sun dancing on roofs of the buildings of Malvern. This is Elgar country and whilst listening to his "Enigma Variations" on the tape cassette, imagine this fine composer writing his works whilst also enjoying the countryside of Worcestershire.

No changes that is apart from the concrete monstrosity of the Worcester A422 Southern Link Bridge downstream from where the River Teme enters the Severn. The bridge has been built high above the river and certainly would not cause any problems to commercial barges working on the Severn during times of flooding. Too much fresh water in the river did cause barges to stop working because they were unable to travel under the bridges due to the lack of air draught. This would be a serious problem in today's commercial world where transport not working for any reason causes a huge financial loss. It would be unthinkable to knock down Worcester Bridge, Mythe Bridge and others, to replace them with large lifting bridges similar to those in Holland. There was plans discussed during the early 1980s to create a Severn Corridor, whereby large commercial barges would sail up the river to Stourport, but this would have entailed rebuilding the locks and altering the course of the river. How would they though, have overcome the problem of navigating through the old bridges?

Upton upon Severn, a sleepy little town totally unchanged apart from a new library, police station and a few modern houses. During Lanchester's visit he noted that cider apples were shipped here and then transferred onto the railway for carriage into the heart of the cider country, Herefordshire. Alas, the railway has long gone and no longer is cider apples shipped here. Instead the only shipment to and from here is people, day trippers enjoying a summer afternoon cruise on the large pleasure boat, "CONWAY CASTLE".

Since leaving Bewdley not many roads follow the course of the Severn, a good map is required to help find the small road that will lead down to the river. Alternatively with a stout pair of walking boots it is possible to walk along the bank of the river, a walk known as the "Severn Way" is continually being developed. One interesting village to pass through is Ripple, scene of the last Royalist victory in the Civil War. The site of the battle is not far from where the Queenhill M50 Motorway Bridge crosses the Severn, certainly more noisy than any Royalist battle would have been.

Soon the river passes beneath one of the finest bridges that cross the Severn, Telford's Mythe Bridge at Tewkesbury. Built with a 170 foot cast iron span, it was opened in 1826 as a toll bridge and Thomas Telford himself is

Mythe Bridge

- 23 -

recorded as once saying "I reckon this the handsomest bridge which has been built under my direction". Unfortunately the constant use of heavy traffic on it has taken its toll and during 1993/4 major repair work was undertaken with the bridge now reopened, but reduced the traffic to one carriageway.

Immediately after passing through Mythe Bridge is the large,modern Mythe Water Works of Severn and Trent. This water treatment plant extracts up to 125,000,000 litres of water per day for use by consumers in the Cheltenham and Gloucester area. There are at several locations on the course of the Severn above Tewkesbury other water extraction plants to serve towns like Coventry and Stafford

Tewkesbury Abbey
from across the Severn

Tewkesbury itself does not lie on the Severn, it's the River Avon that has that distinction. The Avon enters the Severn at two locations, the first is shortly after passing Mythe Water Works, the other about a mile below Upper Lode Lock. The word lode has a special meaning, in the days before the river was canalized it referred to a place where there was a ford, for example Lower Lode, Framilode, Saxon Lode and Wainlode.

Allied Mills have a large flour mill at Tewkesbury and operate a couple of large grain barges. These 43 metre long barges load wheat at either Sharpness or Gloucester and make the three hour trip upriver, through Upper Lode Lock and finally into the River Avon where they discharge their cargo into the mill. Commercially it is only just viable to operate and run the grain barges against the competition from road transport, obviously the one who offers the cheapest rate wins.

Grain barge "Chaceley", one of a pair of the only two commercial barges working on the River Severn

Lanchester only gives a brief mention of what he has seen between Upper Lode and Gloucester, yet another change in the river is about to take place. Soon the river becomes tidal and it's effect can be seen up as far as Upper Lode. One subject not referred in his book is the wildlife on the Severn, yet it has played a big part for man from the past to the present. Today anglers are a common sight, with many fishing clubs staking a claim to land on either bank all the way up the course of the river. During April and May the river becomes alive at night between below Gloucester and up as far as Tewkesbury with elver fishermen. These tiny eel larvae have travelled for three years across from the Sargasso Sea to the Severn, to be fished by men with strange shaped nets on the end of a long pole! Countless thousands are caught and sold to elver stations who in turn export them to Japan and Europe for the re-stocking of their waters. Up until about ten years ago they were a local delicacy, cheap and plentiful, sold by the pint in markets and public houses. Commercialism has taken over and the housewife has been outpriced, even the annual elver eating contest at Frampton on Severn has come to an end.

Villages below Upper Lode at Tewkesbury are liable to suffer from flooding each year. On the side of the boathouse at Lower Lode is the flood-mark for 1947, a particular bad year, in fact the highest this century. All along the length of the Severn nature has provided a natural floodplain, an area where excess water from the river can drain into as flood water tops the river bank. Unfortunately people think they can beat nature and build on these plains, sometimes with dire consequences for each time something large is built on them the water is forced to go somewhere else. Locals who live in the Severnside villages of Deerhurst, Tirley and Ashleworth expect to get flooded and are ready and waiting with sandbags at the bottom of doors and the furniture moved to upper floors.

Half way between Tewkesbury and Gloucester is Haw Bridge. One dark and windy night, five days before Christmas in 1958, a tanker barge was coming down river empty with the river at a high level when on passing under the bridge part of the superstructure caught a girder and consequently brought the structure down onto the barge, killing the skipper. The Army built a temporary Bailey Bridge until the present bridge was opened in 1961.

Below Haw Bridge on the left bank is the Red Lion public house at Wainlodes, complete with tall cliff, this is Gloucester's answer to the seaside. For centuries families with their children on hot summer days have flocked here in their hundreds, children bathing in the river whilst the adults enjoyed the ale at the inn. Thankfully bathing in the Severn is not recommended now and few people indulge in this pastime, preferring instead the cleanliness of the corporation swimming pool. Even today with the nearest seaside accessible within a couple of hours by car, Wainlodes still attracts crowds of people.

Three miles above Gloucester the Severn divides at a point known as the Upper Parting and a mile below the city rejoins again at the Lower Parting. The left or East Channel is the navigation channel and centuries ago was referred to as The Little Severn. The West Channel passes through the village of Maisemore, under Telford's now preserved Over Bridge before meeting at the Lower Parting, a much more prettier route than the East Channel.

The East Channel is very narrow with some tight S bends in it, especially near to Gloucester above Westgate Bridge. Navigating a 43 metre long barge up or down the river here is not easy. Gloucester Lock has to have some control on the movement of vessels and whilst a barge is coming downriver, nothing must be going up. Many a barge has come to grief outside Gloucester Lock whilst attempting to steer into the narrow lock, as there is a strong river current pulling across the entrance towards the Lower Parting. Once safely in the lock the outer gates are closed and the vessel rises up to the level of the water in Gloucester Docks as the lock is filled.

From Gloucester down to Sharpness the Severn is very treacherous for river craft, so it was after many years of construction that the Gloucester and Sharpness Ship Canal was opened in 1827. Before the opening of the canal ships did navigate the Severn up to Gloucester and to overcome the weir at the Lower Parting had to use a large lock which had been built in 1870. The last craft to use this lock is recorded as going through in 1924 and since then the structure has become derelict, although the lock-keepers house is still occupied.

Lanchester in his book has a couple of drawings of Gloucester, sailing ships in the docks, narrow boats on the Quay, Gloucester Bridge which is obviously the old Westgate Bridge, demolished in 1941 and replaced with a temporary bridge, albeit lasting 33 years until 1974 when three new bridges were built there. At Gloucester Lanchester would have seen six bridges over the river, now there are ten, with even more planned when the final link is built on the outer city ring-road.

Gloucester is an ideal city in which to stop at a guest house or hotel whilst exploring the river down the estuary to the Bristol Channel. As with most towns we have passed through, Gloucester has an excellent tourist office, full of information for the traveller. The docks now hosts the National Waterways Museum at the Llanthony Warehouse, well worth a visit.

Chapter Six
GLOUCESTER TO THE BRISTOL CHANNEL

It has to be said, the most unattractive part of the whole length of the River Severn is from three miles above Gloucester to three miles below the city. This is not the Town Council, or anyone else's fault, but the nature of the river, at the limit of the tidal range silt is brought up twice a day and deposited along this reach. Strangers to the town believe the Severn to be a dirty river, not a fair criticism, unfortunately the brown colour of the silt gives it that unclean look.

Before leaving Gloucester it is worth a visit to Over, approximately two miles from the city centre on the road along the causeway over Westgate Bridge. No one is sure of the pronunciation of this strange name, is it "Over" or "Oover", either is accepted by the locals! Between Maisemore Bridge and Over Bridge is where the Gloucestershire and Herefordshire Canal

Over railway bridge
Gloucester

entered the Severn, unfortunately not a lot left here to remind us of this waterway, apart from an old building in the grounds of the now disused Over Hospital.

From where the river splits at the Upper Parting to where it rejoins again at the Lower Parting it forms an island of about three square miles, known as Alney Island. Across the river from Gloucester Lock on the island, Castle Meads coal fired power station was built during the early part of the last war. It was demolished a long time ago to make way for three nuclear powered stations built on the Severn Estuary and Bristol Channel, now the only reminder is the car park built for council workers in the city.

Strange that a county the size of Gloucestershire should have three distinct areas, the Cotswolds, Forest of Dean and Severn Vale, all as different as chalk and cheese. There is no present day link between the Cotswolds and the Severn, which leaves the other two areas being split by the river. Before leaving Gloucester the visitor has to decide which side of the river to go on, for soon the river will widen to almost a mile across. Whichever route is chosen both sides can be explored by simply driving across the Severn Suspension Bridge and returning to Gloucester on the opposite bank. The A38 trunk road travels down what is classed as the English side of the river, from Gloucester towards Bristol and the A48 leads to Chepstow on the Welsh side. passing close to the Forest of Dean on its route.

From the Lower Parting near Hempsted it is possible to walk along the bank of the river, but be warned, the path leads alongside the council refuse tip. The smell of methane gas is quite strong, the sound of gulls screeching as they scavenge from the waste and waste paper clinging to the perimeter fence, not a pretty sight. Opened in 1962, two thousand tonnes of waste is dumped here each day and the anticipated life-span is of another fifteen years. A little farther on past the tip is Netheridge Sewage Works, recently modernized to bring it up to E.E.C. standards, an undisclosed amount of treated sewage is discharged into the Severn, although to the casual visitor this is not noticeable.

The river is tidal up to here as can be seen from the wet sides of the banks between tides, definitely a change in the pattern of the River Severn.

Walking down the field from the top of the Lower Rea the river suddenly becomes beautiful again, not the beauty of the upper reaches of the Severn, but a raw, moody look. The river from here on down is treacherous, very strong currents and quick sands, many a good man has lost his life through not respecting its ugly moods. Shortly Elmore Back is in sight, here and at Minsterworth on the opposite bank is a favourite spot to watch the Severn Bore from. Today the local press make much out of this phenomenon, but it has been happening for countless centuries, since the river began flowing down to the Bristol Channel. From the Atlantic the sea is travelling towards Europe at a very fast speed, slowing down two hundred miles from our shores as it closes towards the Bristol Channel. As it speeds up the ever narrowing funnel of the Bristol Channel and Severn Estuary the flow has to increase in height to accommodate the decreasing width, from a hundred miles to less than five below the Severn Bridge. This forces the height of the flow to fifty feet, the second highest rise of tide in the world. This mass of water surges on up the river until it reaches the weirs at Gloucester, occurring about two hundred and sixty times a year on what is referred to as Spring Tides, nothing to do with our spring season though! Thousands of people line the banks each year to witness this spectacle, some come away quite disappointed, as a good bore depends on many factors, wind speed and direction and river levels being just two. A good bore will produce a wave of about nine feet, but the average is four foot high in the middle of the river. Take care as to where you stand to watch it, as well as getting wet feet, the car can suffer from filling up with water if left in the wrong spot, for immediately after the first wave has passed the river, very quickly, fills up with water.

Lanchester does not say too much about the Severn as it travels on down to the estuary, no doubt for one good reason, roads, or rather the lack of them. Today with the fast car it is possible to drive to various spots and walk along the recognized footpaths, but this is something fairly new. In his day there would not have been these walks with guide books and marker posts leading the way, walking has now become a very popular and enjoyable pastime.

At Longney sands the river begins to suddenly widen with mud flats becoming more visible at low water. Over a century ago the Severn trow could be seen on the river making its way slowly upriver to Gloucester and beyond, if they were fortunate they may have made the city in one tide, but it would take two to come back down. It was for this reason and because the river was so unpredictable that the ship canal was built and subsequently Sharpness Docks. These vessels would bring coal from the Forest of Dean, loading at places like Lydney and Bullo Pill for unloading on the English side at places like Littleton on Severn and Framilode.

Framilode was where the now derelict Stroudwater canal entered the Severn, once a small riverside port.

Leaving Framilode the river begins to form the large Horseshoe Bend, a nine mile length of river leading into a stretch of water known as The Noose, near to Frampton upon Severn. Brunel had a scheme in 1844 of building a canal across the Arlingham peninsula from Framilode to Hock Crib. Perhaps it was never built because of the severe flooding that this piece of land used to be subjected to?

From below Gloucester right down the river as far as Severn Beach the banks have been artificially raised to stop serious flooding of the surrounding area. Even that is not enough and now workmen are slowly rebuilding the banks by the use of small red bricks, now what was a splendid view of the river at Epney has been spoilt by this high,long ugly wall. Whilst this work is taking place the official public right of way does alter making access that bit harder.

Placenames such as Water's End and New Grounds are mentioned by Lanchester, but what he would not have known is that in 1946 at New Grounds the late Sir Peter Scott began the Slimbridge Wildfowl Trust. From this small naturalists site it grew to what we have today, the Slimbridge Wildfowl and Wetlands Trust, not just in Gloucestershire, but at other locations in the country. Well worth a visit, for the enthusiast of wildlife and the casual observer, all tastes are catered for.

Shipbreaking is not a feature of the Severn, but during the last fifteen years two large coasters have been scrapped on the river. Below Newnham on Severn is a tiny inlet called Collow Pill, here a coaster with a dubious past was cut up amongst the trees, now in its place lay a wartime MTB, with enthusiasts trying to salvage it from the mud. Outside of the pill, lying on the banks of the Severn lay several ships of different types, sand dredgers, tankers, tugs and a World War II water carrier. Fred Larkham, well known for his expertise on working on the Severn and Wye, has a fleet of vessels which assisted with the construction of the Second Severn Crossing. In 1985 a large coaster, the ANRO PIONEER was towed from Sharpness to Westbury on Severn by Fred Larkham with one of his tugs to lay on the bank while a decision was made as to what to do with the ship. The owner of the ship secured a deal with someone and the vessel was towed once again down the river, this time to Bullo Pill, where she was finally cut up for scrap whilst laying on the river bank.

Newnham has also witnessed another entrepreneur at work. For many years it had been hoped to build either a bridge or tunnel to cross the Severn from here to Arlingham, but in 1810 these proposals were ruled out as too expensive. In 1939 Enoch Williams, owner of the Aust to Beachley ferry, acquired the ferry rights at Newnham and planned to build a chain ferry. World War II came and the plans were shelved until 1948, but then Williams had a brilliant idea of utilizing old war time floats as a floating bridge across the river. By 1949 he had the hexagonal floats anchored across the Severn, but at each tide they would tilt at a dangerous angle. So the floating bridge was abandoned with the floats being towed away for use by Chepstow Yacht Club.

Commercial salmon fishing, once a flourishing business, is only permitted in the estuary and now only a couple of men are to be seen out in the river. Various methods are used to catch this expensive fish, lave nets, putchers and kipes being the most popular. Standing on the bank at Bullo Pill, if you are lucky, can be seen a lonely figure in a small boat about half a mile off shore. Suddenly this figure will leap out of the boat with his lave net spread high above his head as he runs through the water. For fifty yards he splashes his way forward, when very quickly he gracefully dips the net into the water hoping to have caught a salmon. Without seeing what is in the net the onlooker knows by the disappointing look on his face that his catch of silver has got away. In contrast, salmon are also caught in baskets, to be precise kipe or putcher weirs. Hazel and withy are woven to make the funnel shaped baskets, or putcheons as they are known and when a hundred have been woven they are fastened to stakes running at right angles from the river bank. The salmon is caught as he puts his head into the mouth of the putcheon, unable to withdraw as salmon cannot swim backwards.

Bullo Pill was once a thriving little dock with trows loading coal for places as far away as Ireland. Now this dock is full of mud with a few small cruisers precariously lying against the stone walls, albeit a new set of outer gates have been fitted at the entrance. From here there is a commanding view of the river as it begins to widen very quickly, passing Awre and Gatcombe. The small sombre hamlet of Gatcombe with an attractive red painted house that can be seen for miles from across the river. Sir Francis Drake once stayed here whilst in the Forest of Dean choosing timber for his ships.

Bullo Pill

A little further down the river is Purton, where yet, it is alleged, another great man stayed whilst looking for the best timber for his ships. Sir Walter Raleigh and he stayed at Manor House Farm, the white house which overlooks the Severn. From this Purton look directly across the river and there is another Purton! Why are there two villages with the same name and at similar locations?

Lydney Harbour is now known for its industrial estates, but until thirty years ago was a thriving small port. The dock was built by the Midland & Great Western Joint Railway for the export of coal and timber from the Forest of Dean. The coal was brought in by rail and the wagons tipped their load into the holds of ships waiting below. In latter years timber was imported from Avonmouth in barges full of huge logs for the local plywood factory. Now the dock has been sold to a private company who has plans to develop it into a marina and village. Meanwhile the only commercial vessel to visit is a pleasure steamer on an annual day-trip from here down into the Bristol Channel

Lydney may have suffered from the closure of its dock, but on the opposite side of the river is the thriving port of Sharpness. The dock covers an area of twenty acres and receives ships from all over the world, although due to the present shipping climate these are normally now coasters from the near continent. It is surprising that few people from Gloucestershire ever visit this area on the Severn, admittedly it is not very attractive with its red brick warehouses, stark, tall cranes and general run down appearance. It is worth a visit to witness the skill of the river pilots as they navigate a ship from the estuary, through the piers and into the lock. With the tide sweeping past the entrance at speed he has to put all his skills into practice, no second chance if something should go wrong. And things do go wrong!

The night of 25th October 1960 will never be forgotten. As was normal during those years the river was full of craft of all types coming from Avonmouth and Swansea to dock at Sharpness. Ten o'clock, three miles from the entrance when suddenly a thick fog came down, so thick that skippers were unable even to see the bow of their vessels. Crew men were sent to stand on the bow and listen for other craft as well as the fog siren which was sounding on the end of Sharpness Pier. Barges would be colliding with each other as they swung around to stem the flow of tide before going in between the piers. Two barges had missed the piers and were being carried by the tide towards the Severn Railway Bridge. The WASTDALE H from Avonmouth with a cargo of petrol and the ARKENDALE H from Swansea with a cargo of black heavy oil were locked together with their skippers unable to break their vessels apart.

The first anyone knew of the pending disaster was hearing a dull. strong explosion followed by a huge red fireball, so hot that it cleared a lot of the fog, enabling the other barges to find their way into the lock at Sharpness. Following the accident some brave men carried out heroic acts in trying to rescue crewmen from the tanker barges. When daylight came the full horror could be seen, two spans of the railway bridge had dropped onto the tankers, which still lay smouldering in the river. Five men lost their lives that night with only three being saved, an episode now always referred to as the Severn Bridge Disaster.

This wasn't the only disaster involving tanker barges and the Severn Railway Bridge. Three barges belonging to Severn & Canal Carrying Company were about to enter Sharpness Docks on the 6th February 1939 when something went wrong and all of them were swept upriver. The barges crashed into the bridge pillars and capsized and of the eight crewmen, six were killed. One of the barges, the SEVERN TRAVELLER, is still in use on the Severn, carrying passengers on the river at Worcester.

Lanchester has a fine drawing in his book of the Severn Railway Bridge. Opened in 1879, it was built with twenty one spans of lattice-bow girders and was the first bridge to span the Severn estuary. It was finally demolished in 1968, with only the stone pillars at the side of the ship canal as a reminder of the bridge. The wrecks of the two tanker barges can still be seen lying in the river a few hundred yards upstream from where the bridge once was. A good time to see them is at low water following a large spring tide.

Nuclear power entered the twentieth century with two generating stations opening on the Severn in the 1960s. The first was Berkeley Power Station, but thirty years later this one has already completed its life cycle. Now the building is being demolished, with the reactors having to be encased in concrete for one hundred years! The other nuclear power station is at Oldbury on Severn, both stations now a familiar structure on the landscape.

Between Berkeley Pill and Oldbury on Severn is Sheperdine. Not much here apart from the White House once occupied by the attendant of the navigation light, a superb walk along the foreshore and the Windbound Inn. Following the Severn Bridge Disaster tanker barges were wary of proceeding up to Sharpness in fog, so would lay on the bottom at Sheperdine and wait for the next tide, hoping that the fog would clear. This was a strange sight with big black hulled barges laying side by side in a long row, high out of the water, giving crewmen a chance to inspect their vessels for any damage to the propeller or rudder.

From Sheperdine the navigation channel crosses the river to the Welsh side and it was here that yet another disaster occurred. A dark night in February 1961 and a large tanker barge, the B P EXPLORER, was bound from Swansea to Sharpness. It is alleged that she hit the bottom whilst crossing over from the Welsh side towards Sheperdine and the force of the tide rolled her over, killing all five crewmen. The first anyone knew of this accident was when a worker on the then disused Severn Railway Bridge heard bumping noises and on looking down into the river was shocked to see an upturned hull bouncing through between the pillars. The tanker finally came to rest on the bank at Awre and sometime later was salvaged and towed back to Sharpness.

The vessel was rebuilt and given a new name of B P DRIVER, but after a couple of voyages once more came to grief. This time she ran aground on the rocks at Nash Point in the Bristol Channel, fortunately no one was injured. The barge was finally scrapped, a far too unlucky ship to be rebuilt once more!

Mention has already been made of Littleton on Severn, nothing much here now, but in the days of the Severn trow it was a busy little port with vessels bringing in coal and taking away bricks from the local brick works. This hamlet was made famous in 1887 when a whale became stranded on the mud. Crowds from far afield made the effort to come and see this great large whale lying forlorn and then finally dying. It was then that local entrepreneurs cashed in on this sight by propping open the whale's mouth and charging people to walk inside. When the smell of rotting flesh became too much the whale was taken away to Avonmouth for cutting up.

Another drawing in Lanchester's book illustrates the view from Oldbury church down towards the mouth of the estuary. This same view can be seen today, but now the Severn Suspension Bridge is very much the dominant feature, with the two tall electricity pylons behind it.

Lanchester would never have believed that a bridge could have been built across the river below Littleton, yet majestically the Severn Suspension Bridge graces the skyline as it crosses from Aust to Beachley and, with another bridge crossing the River Wye. Opened in 1966 by Her Majesty Queen Elizabeth II, this fine bridge carries great volumes of traffic on the M48 motorway from England into Wales. Yet now, this bridge cannot cope with today's flow of traffic! Imagine the problem if the bridgebuilders had not been able to build a bridge across the Severn. Before the Severn Bridge traffic had to cross the river by using the ferries operated by Enoch Williams, or face a fifty mile detour around Gloucester. The queues then for the ferry were bad and not without the odd incident. Like cars falling of the jetty whilst negotiating the small ramp onto the ferry and then falling into the Severn!

Most people are aware of the railway tunnel that passes beneath the estuary, but how many know of another tunnel that runs from Beachley to Aust? This modern tunnel was built to carry electricity cables beneath the river and is large enough for men to walk through with ease. The only indication of this is a concrete chamber, surrounded by wire fencing at either end, the Beachley one located not far from the suspension bridge.

Below Beachley point is where the River Wye joins the Severn, strange to think that both rivers have their source within a mile of each other at Plynlimon, the Wye though, taking a direct route to the sea, whilst the Severn chooses to meander. Below where the two rivers meet is the Chapel of St Twrog's, sitting on a very small seaweed covered island a little way off shore. Modern man has taken advantage of this island and fixed a navigation light to it, spoiling the visual effect of this spooky, ancient monument. Although almost nothing is known of the history of the chapel, it is claimed that a man did live here and wanted nothing from his fellow men, only to be left in peace.

From Sudbrook on the Welsh side, passing beneath the English Stones to England is the Severn Railway Tunnel. Opened in 1886, it is thirty feet beneath the river bed and at four and a half miles long, the longest tunnel in Great Britain after the new Channel Tunnel. Each day up to twelve million gallons of water have to be pumped out of the tunnel by the use of giant pumps at Sudbrook. Before the tunnel the rail terminated on a jetty at each side of the river with a ferry service linking them across the New Passage.

One of the largest civil engineering construction sites in the country was located at Severn Beach for the construction of a new bridge with the auspicious title of Second Severn Crossing, hopefully to relieve some of the congestion on the existing Severn Suspension Bridge. Work began in 1992 and the bridge was officially opened in 1996, the total cost estimated at a staggering £270,000,000. This is Britain's longest river bridge with a length of 456 metres. The road is constructed on concrete caissons, with a suspension section over the navigation channel.

Finally, Severn Beach, a small unattractive village which was once advertised in Scotland as one of the West of England's favourite seaside towns! What a shock for them...

We have reached the end of the Severn, or have we? Where does the Severn estuary end and the Bristol Channel begin? People, books or maps, all give different locations, anywhere from the Severn Suspension Bridge to Weston super Mare. Me, I have decided to end the estuary between Avonmouth and Goldcliff.

Until recently the last bridge over the River Severn
now this famous landmark is just the second Severn crossing

Elver fisherman
with his net

CONCLUSION

Who was M Lanchester? Did he travel along other British rivers? No doubt he would be proud to know that someone read his book eighty years later and followed his route down the Severn. Has there been that much of a change from what he saw to the present day? The world has certainly become very modern and thus seemingly a lot smaller, with the latest technology in communications and travel. But the Severn, no, not a lot of physical change, I think Lanchester would recognise most of the landmarks. New buildings there maybe, but the river still winds its long course from the source to the sea.

It is impossible to write everything about the Severn in one book, its history, like its course, is too long. I hope at least, as did Lanchester's From Source to Mouth of 1915, whet your appetite and encourage you to follow the my route from the source to the estuary. Who knows, someone may read this in eighty years time and compare then from now.

And the future, who knows? Can the world keep going at this pace, or will life begin to slow down again. Politicians agree that our roads are now too heavily congested with lorries and that other ways of transporting goods must be looked at. One suggestion has been to get freight back on to rail and rivers. To make that commercially viable the Severn would have to be altered with guaranteed air draught under bridges and sufficient depth of water under the vessels.

To you, the reader of the year of 2077, I hope you have as much pleasure in your journey as I certainly had in mine.

Fly fisherman

ACKNOWLEDGEMENTS

I would like to thank everyone involved in the production of this book. The City of Gloucester Tourist Information Centre, South Staffordshire Water, Gloucester City Museum & Art Gallery, Powys County Council, Gloucestershire County Council, Infrastructure Services of Birmingham, Gloucester City Council, Hereford & Worcester County Council, Gloucester Folk Museum, Llanidloes Tourist Centre, National Power at Ironbridge, Severn & Trent Water, The Environment Agency [EA], Alan Morgan of BBC Radio Gloucestershire, British Waterways, the late Lionel Langford and Dave Moore. Not forgetting of course, my wife Carol, who has been very patient for the last 12 months whilst I have been out and about on my jaunts along the Severn.

NOTE: All the information contained in this book is accurate at the time of going to press. The publishers cannot be held responsible for any information which is found to have changed at a later date.